Seeds! Watching a Seed Grow Into a Plant

Botany for Kids

Children's Agriculture Books

BABY PROFESSOR

EDUCATION KIDS

Speedy Publishing LLC

40 E. Main St. #1156

Newark, DE 19711

www.speedypublishing.com

Copyright 2016

It all started with a seed

A seed is a small embryonic plant covered by a seed coat.

In order for a
seed to grow
into a healthy
plant, it needs
plenty of water
and light.

See how a seed grows into a plant.

The plant starts
life as a seed.

The seed starts
to develop.

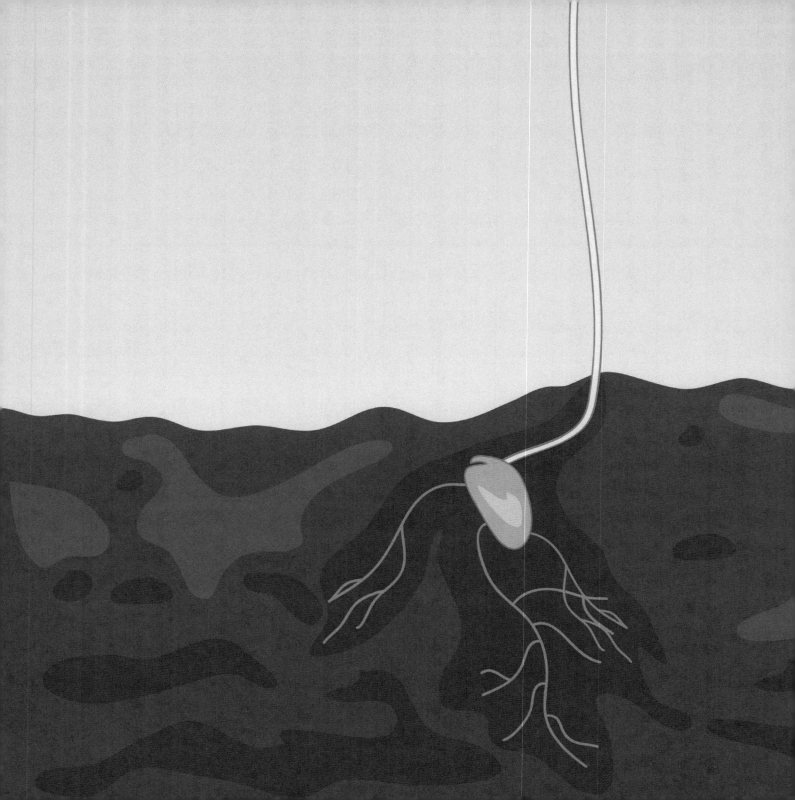

Roots and stem
starts to grow.

Then the leaves slowly start growing.

The plant is starting to produce a flower.

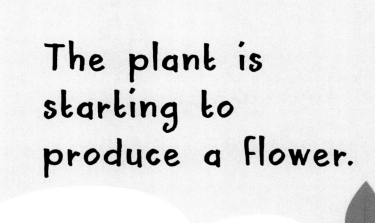

The flower
produces fruit.

The fruit
releases seeds.

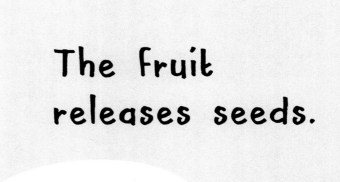

The Life Cycle of a Tree

Seed

Roots

Sprout

Tree

Blooming

Produces Fruits and seeds

Did you enjoy Reading?

You will learn more if you plant a seed by yourself to see how it grows.

Visit

BABY PROFESSOR
EDUCATION KIDS

www.BabyProfessorBooks.com

to download Free Baby Professor eBooks
and view our catalog of new and exciting
Children's Books

Made in United States
Orlando, FL
12 August 2023

36021321R10024